INFINITY

Christopher Thorne

BookLeaf
Publishing

Presentation by *BookLeaf Publishing*

Web: www.bookleafpub.com

E-mail: info@bookleafpub.com

ISBN: 978-93-95784-23-8

First edition 2022

DEDICATION

Mum, for life

Dad…infinite

My bro Yang

Big sis

FAMILY

MC to the core

Home is where the heart is

My friends

My friend (A blood red)

ACKNOWLEDGEMENT

Survivors who stand the test of times

PREFACE

'Infinity'..

Illiterate

You say I'm illiterate this world is oblivious
With oppression, depression & not enough to eat
With our obsession, our expression
to gain & sustain material things, to voice our
thoughts or just let them out
It will prove that nothing like no food or no
sentence or even sense, senseless
about our awareness to this matter it seems like
we are oblivious sometimes decision-less about
what to do next..

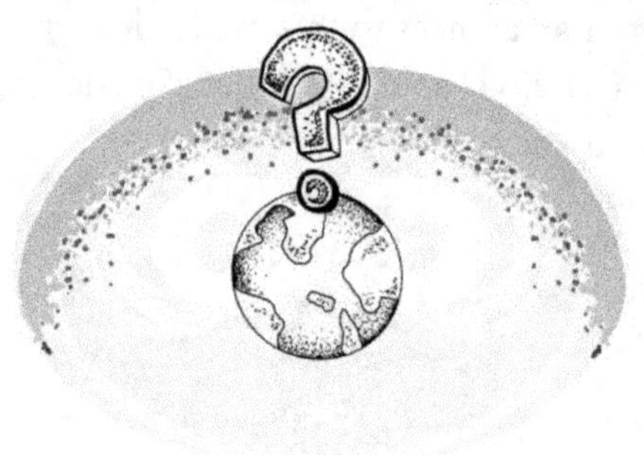

You tell me

You tell me,
What do I do?
Am I doing it right?
Does anyone know?
Does anyone care?
Will anyone help?
I've searched for answers,
Found nothing yet,
I've run for freedom,
Been caught again..
I can't escape the feelings I have,
Too strong,
That's love
That's what I feel for you..

Where? There

Knees shaking,
Trying to walk on a slanted surface,
Looking further off into the distance
Outside flowers are aromatic,
Only my nose in it thus far,
All there is for you to smell is stagnant air
Though I am distant from you, I will take each
step
I am somehow closer,
The day strength
To take each step will be bestowed upon me
Until then it is within my power to continue on
I hope to see you yesterday as another day
passes by
There is no need for a truce,
A broken bond there is yet to be
Though I am sorry for what this place has put
you through
When a new day comes, you'll be stronger.
I am infatuated by you,
Once over the moon,
It all happened too quick
You were taken away too soon,
Please come back
In my thoughts & head,

You're still here with me in my unmade bed.
They tested our love, I wish they had no involvement
Underwhelmed by affirmation's
I'm over it,
Thinking they are so slick,
They have made us sick.
I'm onto you "people" & I too am lying low..
Sweet talk peaches you & I are sweet talkers..
I will not tolerate these night-walkers who have interrupted
Stalking us can't you see we just want to be alone?
So leave us alone to be left alone
A stab at these pricks….
I beg your pardon here's another drip
Donate it to society or you'll leave
Violently,
Knees sturdy..

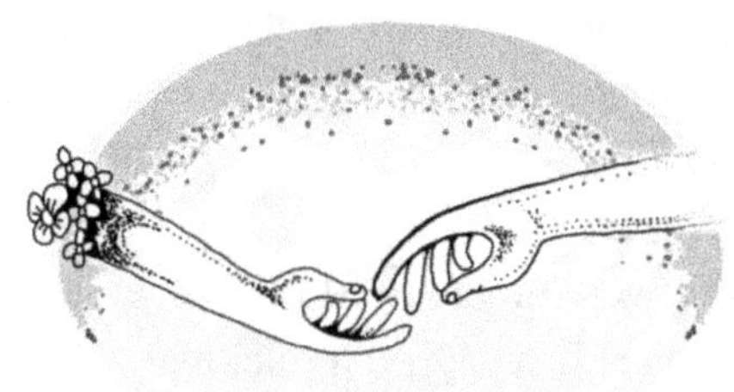

Indefinitely

It was nothing but nonsense,
Nonsensical..
It was all but trivial, trivially..
It was free & wild
At the same time, tame.
Our voice was shared & spoke
Our feelings were communicated
Which were felt
Without a touch,
Nor something to rush
Messages were dealt
Some of it were quite heartfelt
A lot of it was just saying it out
Aloud for once
For once, I'm allowed..
A brief moment of doubt,
Disregarded & excused
We've got nothing to lose
For these thoughts
I'd much rather refuse
& to feel this feeling
I'd much rather say no,
I shouldn't just let it be
Nor come & go,
Though it can surely leave..

Doubt that is,
My voice will stay
You'll hear my voice indefinitely
I'll clean up & tidy every day
Our minds are cluttering
Because it's much easier to love
Than to hate one another
For all the talking
There's so much left
We've yet to say
So I hope I have you as a friend
For at least another day
You can hear me talk
I can listen to you
Your voice & breath will not wander a stray
For at least another day,
You'll always have me as a friend..

indefinitely

Words to action

Contradictions
I contradict the words I say
A part of me likes it this way
I highly dislike it
Sounds like nonsense
Sounds heavenly
Makes perfect sense
Sounds hellacious.
All the self talk & negativity
I contradict it, I like it this way
I'm positively sure
I hate it this way
I have no idea
All the shame & fear
Blood & guts
Safety concerns
No concerns about safety
I contradict it
I like it this way
I walk & talk accordingly
I don't know what to say
Uncoordinated
Whilst with
Perfect coordination
I keep talking
No distractions
Distracted
Silent..

FREE
SPEECH

Before the gate (The naughty corner)

"Back in the box you are, my lizard pets..."
We only witness daylight on your command
The soil & grass we can only touch with your
permission
Roam free when you let us be, one by one, you'll let
us out
You can count the scars here from the inside out.
We should've been nicer, we could've been kind..
Now this after-life is frightening..
Don't fret, my lizard pets,
Fear doesn't live here,
Almost everyone says it's fun, fun, fun & for some
that's already a guarantee
But for now you know where you belong
For what you have done,
You slithering thing as you go
If you repent your sin & figure out your own scarred
skin,
Our time for fun has just begun,
But you can wait,
Perhaps at 8 you can see the sun past the gate
But for now I'll shut the box, you know why, so
figure it out & remember why
For now, you must wait, in the box, it's lights out
You'll only see the light of our beautiful sun when
you shed some light

on your own wrong doings,
So look back in hindsight & figure it out &
momentarily I might let you out
But it's come back when I say, for today you've had
your play,
We'll see what tomorrow brings as it's a new day
We should've withdrew our men, stopped all the
fighting
Our weaponized skin once controlled men, but now
we're controlled by them,
For controlling men
For inflicting pain, I feel all the shame
Out you've come! So out you come
For the rest of you it's back in the dark,
Back in the box for one day you will roam again,
Freely yes,
When of course, I let you go, so let yourselves be
With your once-metamorphosing skin,
This box & the pain you now feel within & without
A scale on your skin that bleeds within.
A scale you need to weigh up, to be whole again
You must wait until your time in the dark is up.
You go back to the box with your lizard friends.
Until the days of conviction leave your relentless
scarred & scale skin..

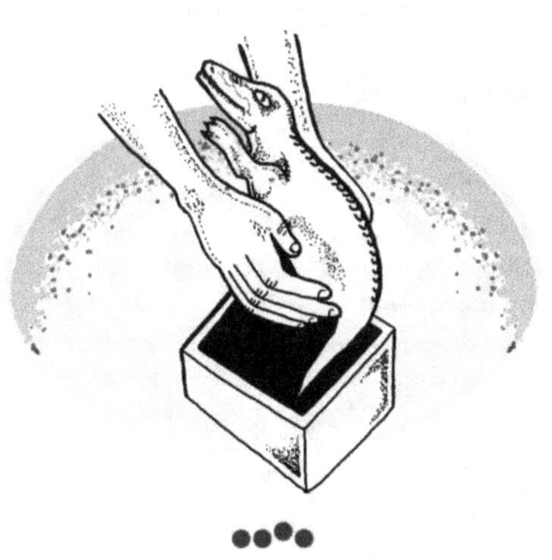

God like

Right knee cap
You're the wrong one
I'm divine
I'm one in my own world.
I know where I am
I know where I belong
As I throw the glass to my left hand
A risky move
There's much to lose
Not a drip escapes
I am the fluent one
Gain access
My personality is on the line
My on line personality
You only see me online
What's on the line
My online personality was in line
You will only see me in line
Days to come
On the line
Up to you
Societies anxieties
I denied it see,
Leave me to be
I give them too many ultimatums
They leave me with none
That's why I remain number one..

God like

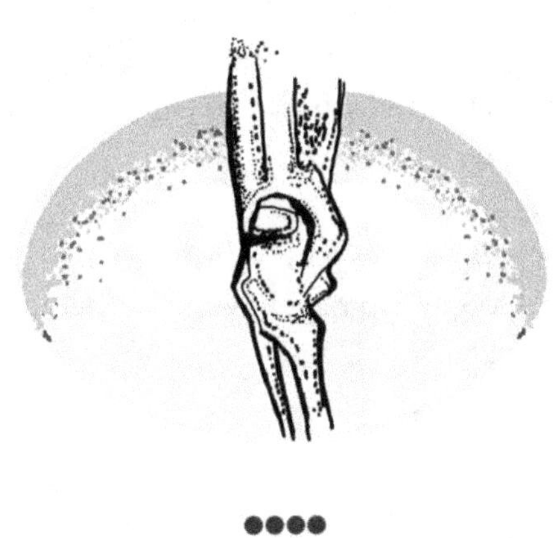

The phone call

What am I doing here?
words I hear muttered every day
Doubt & unfortunate thoughts, thinking you're
to blame
they spread lies surrounding our name..
It's a shame for them I can differentiate
Too bad so sad for some
Take this, take that
Do this, do that
Happily oblige
Until it's too late & they have you where they
want you…
Deeper & deeper
Similar to you
You're not alone
it's called poisoning
Sounds like it's done by a second hand
Like second hand smoking
It's intoxicating
& they're all pushing something & they don't
know what
So vile, So sick, So dim witted
A vile, So some prick.. gets off
Gets off on enhancements

Time dances
But for them it's still life
No age, just gaps
Huge gaps
In societies pages
Funding a war
For a little more
& before we know it
They'll be sitting back
One button to blow it
So I don't care
When really i do
I'm in two minds unlike the hot headed few
But realistically
It's funk you &
Funk you too
I know all the hatred
Won't lead me to places
But what's left to do..
Good gracious
Goodbye

The duplicate

I killed him
Yeah? Yes.
Yeah yeah yeah, With the golden gun?
No the 3D printed replica one
the one I duplicated in my minds eye where this
game resides.
I won.
Surely not the marble stone & bag attached to
the rope
This giant coming towards me
As I swing to throw
The rope, bag & marble stone did not work.
It was all for theatrics.
Or maybe all it did was distract him
As the marble stone bounced off him
Made him mad I have to run, this giant will
swallow me whole
Or squash me with his thumb.
I tripped him on the broken branch, the tree
roots, as I ran
I hoped he would slip & puncture his thick
skin. On a protruding snapped branch
He trips & falls, it took him to the ground, out
cold, My plan is working

As my hand shook as I took aim, After taking
my golden gun with one bullet out
Remember the center of the pupil
Yeah I got it I begin to take the shot. Doubt
filled the air. Would I kill him?
A perfect shot I try to align
Probably why nobody has killed him to this day
I try to pull the trigger as my hand shakes more
I took the shot….

I missed with my one bullet from the golden gun
Our hearts dropped
Well I have come this far, Can't let us down now
So you didn't kill him?
No, I missed, Now watch this
BANG!
Yes, I did. I now have, With a 3D printed gun.
Save it kid he'll only die with the golden gun
You had one shot, missed & you blew it
This giant beast in our purgatory
I know word for word
To this story
I am the chosen one
Here to slay the giant
So instead of a loss I decide to replicate
A bullet & a gun.. Just for fun
Made a 3D printed one
aim to shoot, perfectly aligned
Quicker than you saw me taking

The gun out my newly printed holster
Imaginatively
Straight in the center of the pupil my targets in
line
I take the shot, center of the pupil
It was smack bang in the center, well done
What's next kid? They ask
As nobody has been able to go this far..
In his mouth I enter inside
See those nerve endings, they begin to mutter
As I begin to rip out each nerve ending
How about the two in his brain, that control all
the pain that has been inflicted
I sense I should, It was a fake out, a test
I have to leave them in, or he'd come alive
again.
I left those two the two below I ripped them out
What did you do next?
Walked out & away from his giant dying body
Well done kid.
Oh yeah & I passed the mind games & course
All these mind games that came before, I passed
Theirs, theirs, theirs & theirs
Theirs, theirs & theirs
They, they, those.
Those, them, them. Them, them, those
They, they, those.
& those & them
Ran the obstacle course too

Didn't touch the sides & yeah I fell a few times
But got back up on the run & continued to move
I run this place, can't you see it?
I designed the course
that's why I ran it effortlessly
Well done,
As I commando rolled out the finish line
Yes in hand, those two flags
Says here "only one to have won as you cross
the line"
Go to sleep kid
He's not the chosen one as the voices of doubt
fill the air
Your ancient literature reads one flag to have
won when the chosen one crosses the line,
Well, I had two & I won.
& guess what else I know the air balloon is red
it's all already been depicted in my head
I'm the author & I just rewrote it.
Guessing yet who created this course?
At the top of the box, I jump
My friend in purgatory is a friendly giant.
These are brand-new times now
So let's move on from these two different giants.
as your time here will one day come to an end
Fear & doubt no longer.
A friendly giant awaits you now..

I am the creator

Our inscription

Our inscription,
Our already combusted situation leaves time
faceless,
that means it's gone to heaven, Amen, you got
burnt by the flame now you're disintegrated into
pieces trying to pick it all up, you've got to
detach from the manipulation & put down that
plastic thing that controls the t.v station & turn
to the issue..
while decrypting the subliminal make it a
minimal task to operate & control the media to
use it to your advantage, to plan time ahead of
your heart..

ISSUE

Pull the plug

Pulled the plug on my peers the vacuum turned
off but somehow they all still suck
Spoke without volume

Your best friends a program they've somehow
stuck here
They'll bark if you get too close because they're
dogs through the t.v screen
I don't mean to be mean

On your watch kid
Watch out
no you cannot come in for tea, you're over
stepping the boundaries..

Alone & lonely in an empty bar

Dad alone at the bar he had one drink & 100
years to sit & think..
I bet he was probably told, he could sip it slow,
Or sit & think what got him in this position
I wonder what another would have done,
Downed it in one gulp, barely a buzz with one
glass anyway..
he turned his attention above his left shoulder
with his finger still on the brim of the glass
A t.v yay.
Except it's all black, switched off & lifeless like
dad's ass in that chair
He'd better prepare..
There's a clock on the wall but it's not counting
numbers in a day
it's counting years in a century
As it ticks its hip hip hooray..
He doesn't hear the tickings just an infrequent
ticking.
As the hands move slow..
imagine being told you'd leave a bar in 100
years for the things you've done,
To someday join the other place
I bet you couldn't feel your face

I bet you'd wonder what's the point of taste..
As your head falls & heart drops
"I'm beginning to remember my first born son,
in fact I had two,
I know I had a daughter but I can't remember
her completely yet.."
Thoughts travel through a confused mind at a
slow enough pace
to not feel the emptiness of this space..
"what's gotten me here,
flashbacks & images travel through my mind &
blurry visions"
The voices of trepidation are all that I hear as I
stare at this spirit
I can hear it
I'm alone & scared
Another voice I hear frequent is telling me
"A day at a time, you've got time here, use it
wisely"
One sip, no I mustn't there's thoughts to figure
out
& I've got time to enjoy the thought of it before
it's finished..
who? what? when? why?
All questions & answers revolve around me,
Creaks of old wood..
but nothing seems surrounding this bar

How'd I get here am I intoxicated as I try to
wake up from this nightmare this cannot be
happening as I really know I'm dead,
living in my minds eye in this mind game,
purgatory?…
lying to myself it seems as I try to wake
I'd love to scream but I'm without a voice,
broken & almost completely still
Almost entirely motionless
These voices just won't shut up
as I try to recall & think what is all this clutter in
my head
A day at a time, you've got time here, use it
wisely
I hear a voice I trust, repeat..

Benevolent one

I was the unfortunate one now I'm the
benevolent one
Previously known as
The regenerative one & his degenerate son
Met somewhere in the middle..

Alone & lonely in an empty bar (30 years later)

The t.v remains off, dad still on the chair,
A glass of spirits not a sip of it, yet..
A little wiser
every detail of the bar intact in his brain while
his eyes are shut
he remembers his daughter
& remembers his two sons..
Now they say when you're gone, they're looking
down at you
If you're still stuck in a bar with 100 years of
isolation & thoughts to recollect
is it still so? With 70 years to go
Dads finger on the brim of the glass wondering
how long this will last..
A sip he contemplates..
Suddenly the t.v begins to flicker, a white
electrical spark, draws life to the t.v
Yay & this time not leading to disappointment..
My son appears on the t.v screen..
What's happening here
Don't you dare fear I'm alive & well
thankfully I was beginning to think, like me you
had come to the brink..
I don't know why I'm here

But suddenly so it appears to us
I needed your help & that was finally clear..
Hi dad, Hi son..
I've tried to reach you countless times, I was
talking to myself..
Likewise
envisioning it were you, Now this time I'm
connecting to you.
there's a piece of paper that suddenly appears,
along with a pen,
Scribble I say
Dad scribbles away
How is this happening I'm drawing in detail
You gifted me in this way now I'm here to return
the favour
See art, it's my favourite favour..
It's Chris, by the way
Yeah I know now, I suddenly remember
everything, how is this happening
I need you! That's how.
The time begins ticking, quicker & quicker
Carry me near & carry me dear the voices of
trepidation disappear
It's time now, for the next place.
The voice I trust, inform me that my time in
purgatory had come to an end
Heavenly Father.
The glass of spirits,
Remains untouched..

Wish upon a star

Caught the A-train
Out of here, ha!
They'll order
Change scope
I didn't wish upon a star
I'm mistaken as it's so far
Soon a blue light & a red light
These children still go to bed with a night light
As they watch what you do under new light
They'll call it news, right?
Wishing upon a dead star bang bright
Then I noticed they took a picture of me in bed
I wonder if years on this planet are getting to my
head
& they know where every missing person is
but they need a lead
This is bloody greed
On foot you'll see me run
Probably flip a bird to the observing ones
Moon you in the moonlight
Come & get me
This place has gone for me anyway
You ruined the fun, good on you
We'll have our way in the next place

When we cross over, but like the convicted few,
you also know
Where you belong
You're basically done
You blew my wish it was a satellite dish
Our turn now to have some fun..

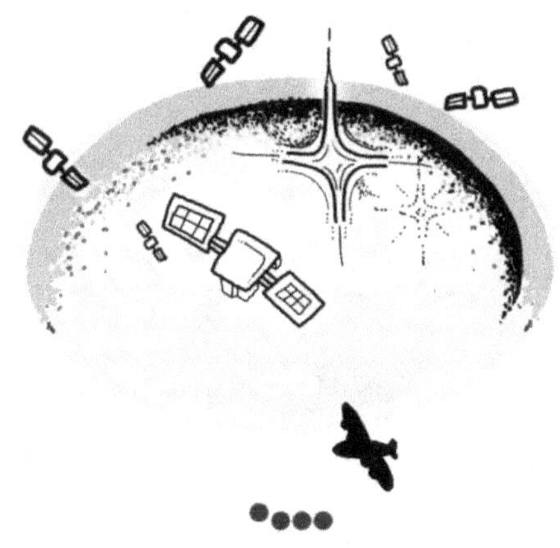

Dept relief

Take a little more
For dept relief
Relieve you of your debt
Here to debt collect
What you owe me as I sit back & watch you
Show me, what you're made of..

Scrambled eggs

41

Scrambled eggs no burnt toast, this toast to you
meant the most, gross news articles sit in car
washes read the garbage amusing technologies
can't stray sit & pray that we'll feel more
connected life's got me feeling gifted,
feel what it's like to lose connection,
disconnection, reconnection, connected.
Span your complex mind & perfect, master your
art & dismiss the lies,
Try cry, pain cries, love lost, love leaves, leave
lost…
Stray away from the inevitable fate because
you're beyond it..

NEWS

••••

The sweet spot

43

Like the candy store
all the flavours
& all that you can taste
Try it
Like 2:22
The first time I tasted you
But you're sweeter than candy
Infinite possibilities when I looked at you..
we touched, touched
It was a rush, rush
Hearts beat, beat
our blood pressure rose, rose..

Humoured it through to you

To beat you
to have humoured it through to you
to beat you to the punch
because it's either knock them out
or take a fall & get knocked out
pick you up number one
I'm here to have won.
Call me out, sit & doubt
point your finger
"yeah that's him"
as I contemplate knocking them out,
because I was out numbered in grave danger, first
punch spectacular!
the rest weren't so particular..
it all happened so quick
Left them dry they wonder why they would've even
tempted this guy, pick him up number one had all the
time to run, as I'm now here left to contemplate, one
by one, a slim chance cornered with nowhere to run
who's to have won & who's yet to have ran as the rest
run,
I'm now offering friendship on common ground
although we have less in common, sadly now
These actions are quite profound
did I earn your respect or are you still tempting me
asking if I want a little more I wonder no but don't
know what to say as I look them in the eyes I wonder

why I still have no friends amongst these few should
I pick him up
"Don't touch him" we'll do it & as we all walk away
without gaining each others respect
"Thank you for being the exception, yet somehow
you're the only one that has split some skin & felt the
force within"
it was a final blow but fortunately for him there's
more to go
"let's take him home boys that's all for this show…"
I say my goodbye's
now they're wondering why
Why did we even try, why did we test this guy?
Or did the test of your aggression lead to your
depression
I feared for my life so I threw the first punch..
Now the bunch have their friend with roles to
emend..

A major losers grand defeat

Not a moment to think & everything to spare
sink, sunk, thunk, I should've done the third
Except I sank all I had, down the machine…
Click click click, I'm now nowhere to be seen
Except through this void where I'm a winner
I bet all I had here you can take my dinner
What's left but here, where I reside
I wonder what bonus lies beside,
a slim chance at opportunity,
A risk I surely cannot take,
I'll do it anyway to reclaim my loss
loss after loss…with brief moments
I'm on the verge of winning
Nowhere to go home to now
This is my moment to own it,
Bing bing bing finally now a chance to show it
what was coming, I've yet to reclaim
It was but a piss poor light show
I might have to go home now,
oh, wait…there are no refunds
as the chimes & bells still echo on..

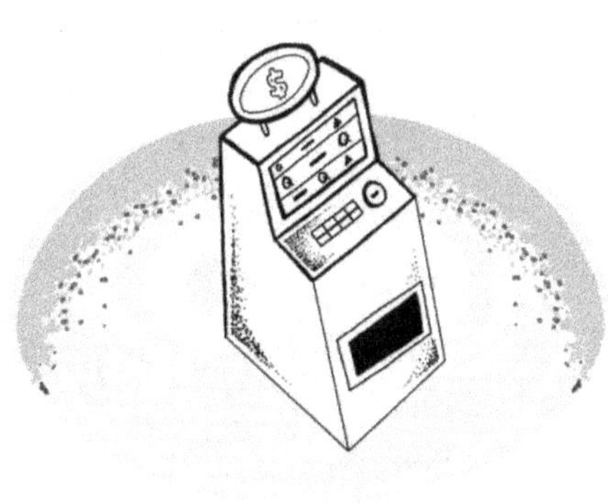

••••

Runners pushing boundaries

I'm not talking name brand sneakers
I'm talking runners & pushers
Somebodies mule
Sit back it's cruel
You're a cog in the machine
somebodies fool
9 to 4 3:51
Headlines
One alone
I won you're done
Hope
torn to pieces saying something unintentionally
Saying it intentionally
Saying it with intention
Yin Yang
Snake & Dragon
Earth
Since birth
Children
Here to save the planet..

Finito..